First World War
and Army of Occupation
War Diary
France, Belgium and Germany

50 DIVISION
151 Infantry Brigade
King's Own (Yorkshire Light Infantry)
1st Battalion
1 July 1918 - 31 May 1919

WO95/2843/1

The Naval & Military Press Ltd
www.nmarchive.com
Published in association with The National Archives

Published by

The Naval & Military Press Ltd

Unit 10 Ridgewood Industrial Park,

Uckfield, East Sussex,

TN22 5QE England

Tel: +44 (0) 1825 749494

www.naval-military-press.com

www.nmarchive.com

This diary has been reprinted in facsimile from the original. Any imperfections are inevitably reproduced and the quality may fall short of modern type and cartographic standards.

© Crown Copyright
Images reproduced by permission of The National Archives, London, England, 2015.

Contents

Document type	Place/Title	Date From	Date To
Heading	WO95/2843/1 1 Bn. KOYLI 1918 July-1919 May		
Heading	War Diary 1st Kings Own Yorkshire Light Infantry July. 1918 Volume II		
War Diary	SS. Odessa	01/07/1918	01/07/1918
War Diary	Taranto	02/07/1918	02/07/1918
War Diary	France	02/07/1918	08/07/1918
War Diary	Martin Eglise	09/07/1918	31/07/1918
Heading	War Diary 1st Kings Own Yorkshire Light Infantry August 1918 Volume 3		
War Diary	Martin Eglise	01/08/1918	31/08/1918
Miscellaneous	1st K.O.Y.L.I. Training Programme-July 21st. to 26th 1918.		
Miscellaneous	1st K.O.Y.L.I. Training Programme-July 29th.-Aug 3rd 1918.		
Miscellaneous	1st K.O.Y.L.I. Training Programme-Aug 12th to 17th 1918.		
Miscellaneous	1st K.O.Y.L.I. Proposed Training Programme For Week Ending 24-8-18	17/08/1918	17/08/1918
Miscellaneous	1st K.O.Y.L.I. Proposed Training Programme For Week Ending August 31st 1918	24/08/1918	24/08/1918
Miscellaneous	1st K.O.Y.L.I.	03/08/1918	03/08/1918
Miscellaneous	1st K.O.Y.L.I. Traning Programme. Aug 5th-Aug 10th 1918.	04/08/1918	04/08/1918
Miscellaneous	1st K.O.Y.L.I. Traning Programme. July 29th-Aug 3rd 1918.	03/08/1918	03/08/1918
Operation(al) Order(s)	Training Operation Order. by Lieut. Col. H. Mallinson D.S.O.	30/08/1918	30/08/1918
Heading	War Diary 1st Kings Own Yorkshire Light Infantry September, 1918 Volume-XXVI		
War Diary	Martin Eglise	01/09/1918	16/09/1918
War Diary	Sus St Leger	16/09/1918	30/09/1918
Heading	War Diary. 1st Kings Own Yorkshire Light Infantry October 1918 Volume-5		
War Diary	Boomerang Wood	01/10/1918	01/10/1918
War Diary	Vaughan's Bank	02/10/1918	02/10/1918
War Diary	Hindenburg Line	03/10/1918	03/10/1918
War Diary	Prospect Hill	03/10/1918	03/10/1918
War Diary	Hindenburg Line	04/10/1918	04/10/1918
War Diary	Richmond Copse	24/10/1918	24/10/1918
War Diary	Hindenburg Line	05/10/1918	05/10/1918
War Diary	Gullamont Farm	06/10/1918	06/10/1918
War Diary	Magquincourt Trench	07/10/1918	07/10/1918
War Diary	Couy.	08/10/1918	08/10/1918
War Diary	Villers Farm	08/10/1918	08/10/1918
War Diary	Vauxhall Quarry	09/10/1918	11/10/1918
War Diary	Meretz	12/10/1918	16/10/1918
War Diary	Escaufort	16/10/1918	16/10/1918
War Diary	Assembly Point	17/10/1918	17/10/1918
War Diary	Railway Emb.	17/10/1918	17/10/1918
War Diary	Objective	17/10/1918	17/10/1918

War Diary	Detraining Pt	17/10/1918	18/10/1918
War Diary	Wessigny Le Cateau Rd	19/10/1918	19/10/1918
War Diary	Avelu	20/10/1918	29/10/1918
War Diary	Maurois	30/10/1918	30/10/1918
War Diary	Le Cateau	31/10/1918	31/10/1918
Heading	War Diary 1st Bn Kings Own Yorkshire Light Infantry November, 1918 Volume 6		
Miscellaneous			
War Diary	Le Cateau	01/11/1918	03/11/1918
War Diary	Bousies Fontaine-on-Bois	04/11/1918	04/11/1918
War Diary	Routbu Pont Rouner	05/11/1918	05/11/1918
War Diary	Hatchette Farm	06/11/1918	06/11/1918
War Diary	Novelles	07/11/1918	07/11/1918
War Diary	Dourlers	08/11/1918	08/11/1918
War Diary	Moncheau	09/11/1918	09/11/1918
War Diary	St. Remy Chausee	10/11/1918	10/11/1918
War Diary	Monchaux	11/11/1918	30/11/1918
Heading	War Diary 1st Bn The Kings Own Yorkshire Light Infantry December 1918 Vol 7		
War Diary	Moncean	01/12/1918	28/12/1918
War Diary	Mecquignies	13/12/1918	13/12/1918
War Diary	Mecquignies	03/12/1918	28/12/1918
War Diary	Mecquignies	11/12/1918	30/12/1918
Heading	War Diary 1st Bn The Kings Own Yorkshire Light Infantry January 1919 Vol 50		
War Diary	Mecquignies	01/01/1919	31/01/1919
Heading	War Diary 1st Kings Own (Yorkshire Light Infantry) 1st to 28th February 1919 Volume II		
War Diary	Mecquignies	01/02/1919	19/02/1919
War Diary	Louvignies Lez Quesnoy	23/02/1919	26/02/1919
War Diary	Louvignies Lez Quesnoy	21/02/1919	26/02/1919
Heading	War Diary Volume 52 March 1919 1st Bn Kings Own Yorkshire L. Infy Vol 10		
War Diary	Louvignies Lez Quesnoy	01/03/1919	31/05/1919

WO 95 2 843/1

1 Bn. KOYLI 1915 JULY - 1919 MAY

WAR DIARY.

1st Kings Own Yorkshire Light Infantry

July, 1918.

Volume —

WAR DIARY or INTELLIGENCE SUMMARY

Army Form C. 2118

(Erase heading not required.)

1/4th The King's Own Yorkshire Light Infantry

July 1918.

Place	Date	Hour	Summary of Events and Information	Remarks and references to Appendices
SS ONESSA	1.	M.30 a.m.	Sailed from ITEA. Very bad accommodation on boat, besides Crew a big French leave party, about 600 troops. Party of 2 French 7 pdrs., shot three rounds before about sunk by 2 British 7.70 pdrs. Very difficult crossing.	H.
TARANTO	2.	3.30 a.m.	Arrived TARANTO and disembarked in lighters by ½ Bn's immediately. Received in Rest Camp all day.	H.
		10.30 p.m.	Bn. entrained at CIMINO STN. Rations, 1 off 93 O.R. details of various units attached for journey. Coys. accommodation good, not very crowded.	H.
	3.	08.30 a.m.	Reported from CIMINO.	H.
		6.30 a.m.	Halt Reggio di BRINDISI.	H.
		8.0 p.m.	Halt Ryan at FOGGIA.	H.
	4.5		Travelling up the East Coast of ITALY and Italian Riviera.	H.
	6.		Crossed frontier into FRANCE.	H.
	7.		Travelling through France.	
	8.		Do Do Rations issued daily whilst on Train.	H.
MARTIN EGLISE	9.	8.30 a.m.	Arrived ARQUES and detrained, proceeded by march route to MARTIN EGLISE and went into Camp No. 141.	H.
	10		Leave renewed by H. OR's per day commenced.	H.
	11		Transport animals and wagons arrived, except 9 chargers.	
	12.		Relieved to remain from 14.7.	
	13.4		Date when lost from 14.7. Bn. inspected by Brig. Genl. A.C. JACKSON MSO Comdg. 50 Div.	
	14th		Bn. Major Carey in 14th July celebrations on the Place, DIEPPE. Genl. Rawlinson Comdg. 4th Army, inspected Bn. trenching.	H.

Army Form C. 2118.

WAR DIARY
or
INTELLIGENCE SUMMARY.

(Erase heading not required.)

July 1918 Sheet 9. 2
1/9th The King's Own Yorkshire L.I.

Place	Date	Hour	Summary of Events and Information	Remarks and references to Appendices
MARTIN ROUSE	July 15.		Bat Returned on leave 14 days UK. 5/Lt Dinsmore Bim POSTED to 151. Supply Rees under Brig Gen. R.E. SUGDEN DSO CMG 1918 A. Roe - 4th K.R.R.C. and Capt. INNISKILLING FUS.	
	16-17.		Capt. R. Meadows on leave UK. 14 days.	
	18		17² Lahertyptes Trained by Bn. on fatigues finishing cable and digging/Aircraft protection.	
	19.		Relieved by Brig Gen R.E. SUGDEN DSO to all Officers and Sergts N.C.Os on "Relay Lighting" Pergusa Church Parade.	
	24.		Training Resumed as per attached programme by 2E INGRAM OC and B/1/4/5.	
	25.		STARLING on leave to UK. 14 days.	
	26.		2/Lt. W. HOWARD and 16 ORs transferred to 151. 2/Lt M. Balton R.W C MILNER C.E and Senior attached to Batt. Return to all officers to see offered by Brig'r on Parade in dep of 2 WM Moon on leave to UK 14 days company Ly lectures to Tranto Dep Leave allotment stopped. Div Sward attended Divisional Church Parade.	
	28.		2/Lt. F. REEVES. and 25 ORs to D.H. Sig School.	
	29.		Training as per other programme. Rus Xy day stand easieved until 10-30 pm all through morning 10-30 pm	
	30		Air Raid about 12-0 am Bombs comparative short distance away.	
	31		2/Lt. CA.R. BROMHAM and 7 ORS to 51 or battery Captain. Compound Bolsheviks Church 7.7 working days 245 daily	
	"		" 10. " D4.co. " P.T. 12. "	
	"		" 10. " D4.co. " Coursese 12. "	
	"		2/Lt. R. PATERSON regained from leave To Hosp. SICK. during month 49 org Capt STOTT died MALARIA 23. " To Conval. 45. " Hosp. 44. " Sch. 52 Forms C2118/14 N. STAFF H/14

Congrats for K.Y.L.I.
M. Mc Cullagh Lt

WAR DIARY

1st King's Own Yorkshire Light Infantry

August 1918.

Vol 3

Volume —

O.40
11 sheets

WAR DIARY
or
INTELLIGENCE SUMMARY.
(Erase heading not required.)

Army Form C. 2118.

August 1918

Place	Date 1918	Hour	Summary of Events and Information	Remarks and references to Appendices
MARTIN EGLISE	Aug 1st		Whole day. The Bn was inspected by Rifm. H.E. Seyler, M.S.O. Boots not issued to the Bn. — Sports met Coy. with football in progress in the afternoon and cleared by The Second Jellin in the Evening. The officer submitted to the Staff in the morning. Capt Morris signed for leave.	
		2	Haverbrook arrived from the J.B.O.	
		6		
		7	Maj J.R.R. Macarthur and Capt R.R.Roberts signed for leave. 2/lt R.W.of	
			awdaux & lyles.	
		8	Captain G.D. Clarke proceeded on leave — re-organisation of the W.O. & Men	
		10	Capt Strother & Mr J. Stills proceeded on leave.	
		11	Lt Hogan to Hove for leave — Col. Hogarth & N.O. officers to Pt.Macdivat lat Btn on his return to Command Base.	
		12	Capt E. Dover Resuming leave — Major Graham'let to Command Base	
		13	Lt Stephen Proceed leave. Brig Packlin R.E. arrived Dir. Cas 61	
		14	2/Lt Ohphila & provisn. tent. Capt. J.R. King arrived & joined for duty Base	
			Lt Roundary Proceeds — leave. Coys and Bn. Cd. reported on trends exercised to extolled &	
		15.	R.Mr. Re Statemarle. to Controllent Camp	
		16	2nd R. D.L.C. W.O.J. Moss Sans on leave.	
		17	Ltlt Gulli and Boulton proceed on leave	
		18	Lt.T. Rimecour, Barker, Rye proved to Base (Capt Heald) arrived	
		19		
		20	Capt. Fitz-Hgh. and L.S.R. Amiens — also wounded to report to L.W.R.	
		21		

Army Form C. 2118.

WAR DIARY
or
INTELLIGENCE SUMMARY.
(Erase heading not required.)

August 1918 Feb 2

Place	Date	Hour	Summary of Events and Information	Remarks and references to Appendices
MERTON ECLUSE	22			
	23			
	24			
	26			
	27			
	28			
	29			
	30			
	31			

1st K.O.Y.L.I.

Training Programme - July 21st. to 26th 1918.

Date.	Time	Locality	Nature of Training
July 22nd	0645-0730	Camp 14 and Foret D'Arque	Gas Training.
	0900-0930	do.	Physical Training
	0945-1045	do.	A & B Coys. Prelim. Musketry. C & D Coys. Close Order Drill
	1130-1215	do.	Bayonet Fighting
	1400-1500	do.	C & D Coys. Prelim. Musketry A & B Coys Close Order Drill Handling Arms.
July 23rd	0645-0730	Camp 14 and Foret D'Arque	Gas Training
	0900-0930	do.	Physical Training.
	0945-1045	Field N.E of Camp.	C & D Coys. Prelim. Musketry
	0945-1045	do.	A & B Coys. Close Order Drill Handling of Arms.
	1130-1215	Camp 14 and Foret D'Arque	Bayonet Fighting
	1400-1500	do.	A. & B Prelim. Musketry. C & D Close Order Drill Handling of Arms
July 24th	0645-0730	Camp 14 and Foret D'Arque	Gas Training.
	0900-0930	do.	Physical Training.
	0945-1045	do	Bayonet Fighting
	1130-1215	do.	Preliminary Musketry.
	1400-1500	Field N.E. of Camp.	Close Order Drill, Handling of Arms.
July 25th.	0645-0730	Camp 14 and Foret D'Arque	Gas Training.
	0900-0930	do.	Physical Training
	0945-1045	do.	A & B Coys. Extended Order C & D Coys. Prelim. Musketry
	1130-1215	do	Bayonet Fighting
	1400-1500	do.	A & B Coys. Prelim. Musketry C & D Coys. Extended Order.
July 26th	0645-0730	Camp 14 and Foret D'Arque	Gas Training
	0900-0930	do.	Physical Training
	0945-1045	Field N.E. of Camp.	A & B Coys. Coy Drill. Marching Order C & D Coys do.
	1130-1215	Camp 14 and Foret D'Arque	Instruction Guards & Sentries
	1400-1500	do.	Preliminary Musketry.
July 27th	0645-0730	Camp 1r and Foret D'Arque	Gas Training
	0900-0930	do.	Physical Training.
	0945 1045	do.	Bayonet Fighting
	1130-1215	do.	Preliminary Musketry.
	1400-1500	Field N.E. of Camp.	A & B Coys. Extended Order Marching Order
	1400-1500	Camp 14 and Foret D'Arque	B & C Coys do.

Training of Signallers, Lewis Gunners, and Stretcher Bearers at same hours
Preliminary Musketry to include Working of Bolts, Rapid Loading, Snapping et

Recapitulation

Gas Training	4½ hrs.		Physical Training	3 hours	
Bayonet Fighting	4¼ "		Prelim. Musketry	5½	do.
Close Order Drill	3 "		Extended Order Drill	2	do.
Company Drill	1 "		Guards & Sentries Instruction in,	1	"

P.T.O.

1st K.O.Y.L.I.
TRAINING PROGRAMME — July 29th – Aug 3rd 1918.

Date	Time	Locality	Nature of Training.
July 29th	0645-0730	Camp 14 and Foret D'Arque and Training Ground.	Gas Training, including 1 Coy firing on 30 yds Range in masks.
	0900-1230	Ground to be Selected	1 Coy short route march & Outpost Scheme. Coy Cmdrs to submit scheme to C.O.
	0900-0930	Camp 14 and Foret D'Arque and Training Ground.	3 Companies Physical Training.
	0945-1045	do.	1. Coy 30 yds. Range. 2 Coys. Company Drill in Marching Order.
	1130-1215	do.	1 Coy. 30 yds Range. 2 Coys. Bayonet Fighting. Rapid Loading and Aiming.
	1400-1500	Camp 14 and Foret D'Arque	Preliminary Musketry, Handling of Arms (2 Coys) 1 Coy. 30 yds Range.
July 30th	0645-0730	Camp 14 and Foret D'Arque	)
	0900-1230	Ground to be selected	) As
	0900-0930	Camp 14 and Foret D'Arque.	) for
	0945-1045	do.	) 29th.
	1139-1215	do.	)
	1400-1500	do.	)
July 31st	0645-0730	As for 30th	As for 29th
	0900-1230	do	do
	0900-1000	do	3 Coys. 20 mons each in turn Physical Training under C.S.M.I. Gumbrell A.G.S. (Preliminary Musketry whilst waiting).
	1015-1045	do	1 Coy under A.G.S. Instructor for Bayonet Fighting. 2 Coys. Rapid Loading and Aiming. Handling of Arms.
	1130-1215	do.	1 Coy 30 yds Range. 2 Coys close order drill
	1400-1500	Training Ground	Extended Order Drill. (Marching Order).
Aug 1st		MINDEN DAY	GENERAL HOLIDAY
Aug 2nd.	0645-1215	As for 29th	As for 29th.
	1400-1500	As for 31st	As for 31st.
Aug 3rd	0645-0730	Camp 14 and Foret D'Arque	Gas Training. 1 Coy on 30 yds Range in masks.
	0900-1230	Route to be selected	Bn. Route March, with scheme.

Training of Lewis Gunners, Signallers and Stretcher Bearers same hours.
Preliminary Musketry to include Rapid Loading, Aiming, Snapping etc., with Bayonets fixed.

RECAPITULATION:-
Gas Training — 3¾ hours
4 Coy. Schemes — 3½ hours
Bn. Route March — 3½ do
Physical Training — 1 hr. 50 min.
Company Drill Each Coy — 1 hr.
Extended Order Each Company — 1 do
Preliminary Musketry — 2 hrs 40 mins.
Bayonet Fighting, Handling of Arms etc ¾ hr. daily

1st K.O.Y.L.I.

Training Programme - Aug 12th to 17th 1918.

Date	Time	Locality	Nature of Training
Aug 12th	0645-0730	Camp 14 and Foret D'Arque	Musketry.
	0900-1230	Greves	2 Coys Combined Outpost Scheme.
		Training Ground	2 Coys. Coy Training, special reference to Fire control & Discipline, employment of runners etc.
	0200-0300	do.	1 Coy. Drill - Close & extended order.
		Bombing Ground	1 Coy. Bombing
		Training Ground	2 Coys. P &B.T. under C.S.M. Campbell A.G.S.
Aug 13th			Working parties and bathing.
		Place to be notified later	Night work for Officers & Senior N.C.Os. (marching on Compass Bearings.
Aug 14th		Place to be notified later.	Bn. Tactical Exercise
			Night work for 2 Coys marching to Assembly Ground
Aug 15th	0645-0730	Camp 14 and Foret D'Arque	Musketry
	0900-1230	Training Ground	2 Coys. Coy Training.
		Place to be notified later.	2 Coys. Outpost Scheme
	0200-0300	Training Ground	2 Coys. P & B.T.
			1 Coy Drill
		Bombing Ground	1 Coy Bombing.
Aug 16th			Working parties and bathing.
		Place to be notified later	Night work for 2 Coys. (marching to Assembly Ground)
Aug 17th		Place to be notified later	Battalion Tactical Exercise.

11-8-18.

Major
Commanding 1st K.O.Y.L.I.

1st K.O.Y.L.I.

Proposed Training Programme for Week Ending 24-8-18.

Date	Time	Locality	Nature of Training.
Aug 19th.	6-45 a.m. to 7-30 a.m.	Camp & Training Field	Musketry.
	9-0 " " 12-30 p.m.	Training Field	Battalion Parade. Gas & Coy. Training. Drill.
	2-0 p.m. " 3-0 p.m.	Bombing Ground Training Field & Camp & 30 yds. Range.	1 Company. Musketry & Specialists' Training, P.T. & B.T.
Aug 20th.	WORK.	Foret D'Arque	Coy. night Schemes with Gas Training.
Aug 21st	6-45 a.m. to 7-30 a.m.	Camp & 30 yds Range	Musketry
	9-00 a.m. to 12-30 p.m.	EASY & CHEDES Camp.	Two Coy. Scheme Platoon & Coy. Training.
	2-0 p.m. to 3-0 p.m.	Camp & 30 yds Range	Musketry & Spec-ists' Training.
Aug 22nd	6-45 a.m. to 7-30 a.m.	Camp, Training Field, & 30 yds Range.	Musketry.
	9-0 a.m. to 12-30 p.m.	Training Field	Battalion Parade-Drill, Gas, & Coy. Training.
	2-0 a.m. to 3-0 p.m.	Bombing Ground Training Field, Camp & 30 yards Range.	1 Company. Musketry & Specialists' Training, P.T. & B.F.
Aug 23rd	WORK.	To be detailed later	Officers & N.C.Os. Night Marching by Compass.
Aug 24th	6-45 a.m. to 7-30 a.m.	Camp.	Cleaning Camp & Renovating Camp equipment.
	9-0 a.m. to 12-0 p.m.	Camp & 30 yds. Range	Musketry, Platoon & Coy. Training.
		Neighbourhood S.E. of ANCOURT	Two Coy. Scheme.

Bombing Ground also allotted to 2 Coys. Monday morning & Thursday morning from 9-30 a.m. to 12-30 p.m.

H.W. Lyne
Captain.
Commanding 1st K.O.Y.L.I.

17-8-18.

1st. K.O.Y.L.I.

Proposed Training Programme for Week Ending August 31st 1918.

Date.	Time.	Locality.	Nature of Training.
26th.	8-30 a.m. to 12-30 p.m.) 2-0 p.m. to 4-0 p.m.)	Long Range. MARTIN) EGLISE - GREGES Rd.)	Musketry.
	6-45 a.m. to 7-30 a.m.) 8-30 a.m. to 12-30 p.m.) 2-0 p.m. to 3-0 p.m.)	Training Field	(Coy., Platoon & (Specialists' Training do.
27th		WORK & BATHING.	
	9-30 p.m.	To be detailed later	Small Coy. Night Scheme
28th.	9-30 a.m. to 12-30 p.m. (	Field Firing Range & Bombing Ground	Field Firing. Bombing.
	7-0 a.m. to 7-0 p.m.	600 yds. Range & Foret D'Arques.	(Musketry & Specialists' (Training.
29th	WORK	CAMP	Making paths & Interior Economy.
	4-0 p.m.	To be detailed later	Battalion Tactical Exer for Officers & N.C.Os.
30th	WORK &	BATHING	
	9-0 p.m.	To be detailed later	Marching on Compass Bearings.
31st.	6-0 a.m.		Brigade Route March.

24th. August 1918.

H.W.Lym

Captain
Commanding 1st K.O.Y.L.I.

1st K.O.Y.L.I.

S C H E M E .... Aug 3rd 1918

Ref. DIEPPE sheet 1/100,000.

GENERAL IDEA

The enemy are advancing down the valleys of the rivers EAULNE and BETHUNE on DIEPPE.

On the night of the 3rd August, the enemy advance guard had taken up a line running approximately through the first S in ST GERMAIN d'ETABLES - the U in ANCOURT - the O in GRAINCOURT.

The 151st Bde. in the centre of the 50th Divn. is holding a front of 1500 yds. on a line running through the B in BOIS d'ARCHELLES - the first R in FORET D'ARQUES - the Q in BRACQUEMONT

SPECIAL IDEA.

The 151st Bde. are taking part in a general attack, and the 1st Bn. K.O.Y.L.I. is ordered to attack on a 700 yds front with its RIGHT resting on, and including the track running N.E. which leaves the MARTIN EGLISE - ST NICOLAS RD due N of the E in FORET D'ARQUES

ZERO hour................10-0 a.m.

Lieutenant.
Acting Adjutant 1st Bn. The King's Own Yorkshire Light Infantry.

2-8-18.

War Diary

1st K.O.Y.L.I.
TRAINING PROGRAMME:— Aug 5th — Aug 10th 1918.

Date	Time	Locality	Nature of Training
Aug 5th	6-45 – 7-30 a.m.	Camp 14 and Foret D'Arques	Musketry.
	8-30 – 9-30 a.m.	do	) Coys at Training, Gas
	9-45 –10-45 a.m.	do	) and Musketry.
	11-31 –12-15 a.m.	do	) B Coys. under C.S.M.I.
	2-0 – 3-0 p.m.	do	) General MGS Gas P and B.T
Aug 6th		Foret D'Arques	For the Coys and Bombing. Night Work for Officers Marching on Compass Bearings.
Aug 7th			Tactical Scheme.
Aug 8th	8-30 –12-30 a.m.	Camp 14 and Foret D'Arques	As for 5th with the exception of D Coy. D. Coy. Outpost Scheme and Route March (Place to be notified later).
Aug 9th		Foret D'Arques	Musketry Parades and Bombing Night Work for Officers, Marching on compass bearings.
Aug 10th	6-45 – 7-30 a.m.	Camp 14 and Foret D'Arques	Gas & Musketry.
	9-0 –12-30 a.m.	Foret D'Arques	Bn. Route March with Scheme.

Training of Specialists at same hours

J. Blanshard Lt.
a/Adjt.
1/K.O.Y.L.I.

4-8-18.

1st K.O.Y.L.I.
TRAINING PROGRAMME — July 29th – Aug 3rd 1918.

Date	Time	Locality	Nature of Training.
July 29th	0645–0730	Camp 14 and Foret D'Arque and Training Ground.	Gas Training, including 1 Coy firing on 30 yds Range in masks.
	0900–1230	Ground to be Selected	1 Coy short route march & Outpost Scheme. Coy Cmdrs to submit scheme to C.O.
	0900–0930	Camp 14 and Foret D'Arque and Training Ground.	3 Companies Physical Training.
	0945–1045	do.	1. Coy 30 yds. Range. 2 Coys. Company Drill in Marching Order.
	1130–1215	do.	1 Coy. 30 yds Range. 2 Coys. Bayonet Fighting. Rapid Loading and Aiming.
	1400–1500	Camp 14 and Foret D'Arque	Preliminary Musketry, Handling of Arms (2 Coys) 1 Coy. 30 yds Range.
July 30th	0645–0730	Camp 14 and Foret D'Arque	)
	0900–1230	Ground to be selected	) As
	0900–0930	Camp 14 and Foret D'Arque.	) for
	0945–1045	do.	) 29th.
	1139–1215	do.	)
	1400–1500	do.	)
July 31st	0645–0730	As for 30th	As for 29th
	0900–1230	do	do
	0900–1000	do	3 Coys. 20 mons each in turn Physical Training under C.S.M.I. Gumbrell A.G.S. (Preliminary Musketry whilst waiting).
	1015–1045	do	1 Coy under A.G.S. Instructor for Bayonet Fighting. 2 Coys. Rapid Loading and Aiming. Handling of Arms.
	1130–1215	do.	1 Coy 30 yds Range. 2 Coys close order drill
	1400–1500	Training Ground	Extended Order Drill. (Marching Order)
Aug 1st		MINDEN DAY	GENERAL HOLIDAY
Aug 2nd.	0645–1215	As for 29th	As for 29th.
	1400–1500	As for 31st	As for 31st.
Aug 3rd	0645–0730	Camp 14 and Foret D'Arque	Gas Training. 1 Coy on 30 yds Range in masks.
	0900–1230	Route to be selected	Bn. Route March, with scheme.

Training of Lewis Gunners, Signallers and Stretcher Bearers same hours.
Preliminary Musketry to include Rapid Loading, Aiming, Snapping etc., with Bayonets fixed.

RECAPITULATION:—

Gas Training	3½ hours	
4 Coy. Schemes &a.	3½ hours	
Bn. Route March	3½ do	
Physical Training	1 hr. 50 min.	
Company Drill Each Coy	1 hr.	
Extended Order Each Company	1 do	
Preliminary Musketry	2 hrs 40 mins	
Bayonet Fighting, Handling of Arms etc	½ hr. daily	

SECRET.
Copy No......

Training Operation Order.
by
Lieut. Col. H. MALLINSON D.S.O.

Ref. DIEPPE Sheet, 1/100,000.
August 30th 1918.

	1.	Brigade in conjunction with troops on both flanks will attack at 3-30 a.m. August 31st.
Front and Objective.	2.	**Right Boundary** - VARENNE - ST GERMAIN D'ETABLES Rd (inclusive).
		Left Boundary - The R. BETHUNE to where it crosses DOMPIERRE-ECREMESNIL Rd. thence a due N. and S. line.
		Objective - ST. GERMAIN D'ETABLES and Road running S.E. from it through EU in MEUSE.
Distribution	3.	4th K.R.R.C. will clear area up to line of re-entrant shown under words LES ETRUISSARTS and projection of this line in due Easterly direction to DOMPIERRE - FREULLEVILLE Road (inclusive) W. of River BETHUNE. White Very Lights will be fired when objective is gained.
		Formation - 3 Companies in F.L. in 2 waves at distance of 50 yards.
		1 Company in support in Artillery formation 100 yards behind 2nd wave.
		1st K.O.Y.L.I. (on Right) and 6th R. Innis Fus. will advance at zero, and conform to the front of the final objective of 4th K.R.R.C. and when White Very Lights are fired will pass through 4th K.R.R.C. and capture final objective.
		Inter Battalion Boundary. - line through 3rd S in LES ETRUISSARTS and R in ST. GERMAIN D'ETABLES
		Formation. - for advance to 1st objective, Artillery formation.
		for advance from 1st Objective - 2 Companies in F.L. in 2 waves at 50 yards distance.
		2 Companies in support 100 yards behind 2nd wave in Artillery formation.
Assembly.	4.	Assembly area is formed approx. by VARENNE - ST. AUBIN Rd. (between VARENNE and R. BETHUNE) and line drawn parallel to and 200 yards East of this Road.
		4th K.R.R.C. will form up with 1st wave on kicking off tape - 1st K.O.Y.L.I. and 6th R. Innis Fus in rear of 4th K.R.R.C.
	5.	The Bn. will parade at 8-10 p.m. on 31st August: Dress:- Fighting Order.
		Order of March: A., B., C., D., H.Q.
		Lewis Gun Limbers & Pack Animals as detailed will march in rear of Coys. as usual.
		the Bn. (Continued)

as usual.

(2).

The Bn. will march to Point A "First road junction S.E. of MARTIGNY on MARTIGNY - VARENNE Rd", via ARCHELLES - ARQUES - MARTIGNY - VARENNE.

6. The Bn. Intelligence Officer will reconnoitre road from Point A to Point B. ("Second Road junction S.E. of MARTIGNY").
He will also arrange to mark out the ground showing where each Platoon will rest when in the assembly formation. For this purpose the following will be detailed to parade under the Bn. Intelligence Officer at 6-15 p.m. on 31st August.
1 Officer, 2 N.C.Os. and 2 men per Coy.
2 N.C.Os. and 1 Orderly by Bn. Hd.Qrs.

7. Formation. The Bn. will form up at the point of assembly (ref para 4) as follows:-
A and B. Coy. in front line - C and D in support in Artillery Formation. 2 Platoons of each Coy in Front Line, 2 platoons in support.
Each Coy is allowed a frontage of 160 paces with a depth of 56 paces.
The right of B. and D. Coy will rest on VARENNE - ST GERMAIN D'ETABLES Rd and the left of A and C will rest approximately on road junction at Top of N in NOVILLE
Os. C. A and C are responsible that close touch is maintained with 6th R. Innis Fus. on the left.
No troops will be on the Western side of VARENNE - ST AUBIN -le- Cauf Rd.

8. The Bn. Intelligence Officer will meet the Bn. at Point A with Bn. Guides (as detailed), and will guide the Bn. to point B, where Company Guides will be. At this point Lewis Gun Limbers will be off-loaded, pack animals will assemble in rear of column.
Coys. will then be guided by their own Coy. Guides to point of assembly at 5 minutes interval.
Bn. H.Q. will follow the rear Coy. and will be taken to Bn. H.Q. at TALL POPLAR near Cross Roads S.W. of N in NOVILLE
An Orderly will be detailed by the Bn. I.O. to guide Pack Animals to Bn. H.Q. by the road. Limbers will remain at point "B".

9. Coy. Comdrs. will report to Bn. H.Q. when in position, Os. C. A and C will also state in their report that touch has been gained with Bn. on left.

10. On conclusion of operations Coys. will form up on the VARENNE - ST AUBIN - le -Cauf Road in fours facing N.W. Limbers will then move from point B to be reloaded. On completion of loading Coys will then march home independently via ST AUBIN -le- Cauf through FORET D'ARQUES.

Captain.
Adjutant 1st K.O.Y.L.I.

Aug 30th 1918.

WAR DIARY

1st King's Own Yorkshire Light Infantry

September, 1918

Volume — XXVI

Army Form C. 2118.

WAR DIARY
or
INTELLIGENCE SUMMARY.

1st Bn. THE KING'S OWN (YORKSHIRE LIGHT INFANTRY).

Volume XXVI September 1918.

(Erase heading not required.)

Place	Date Sept.	Hour	Summary of Events and Information	Remarks and references to Appendices
MARTIN EGLISE	1st		Captain H.K. Lambert proceeded to Hd. Qrs. 151 Infy. Bde. for temporary duty.	033
	3rd		Bn. on working parties &c.	033
	4th		Captain T.H.J. Upton proceeded to Div. Rest Station.	033
			Bn. took part in Divl. Route March.	
	5th		Lt. H.B. Judge rejoined from leave.	033
	6th		Platoon & Coy. Training.	033
	7th		do	033
			Bn. inspected by Maj. Gen. H.C. Jackson, D.S.O. Comdg 50th Division.	
	8th		Lt. H.B. Judge admitted to Fd. Ambulance sick.	033
	10th		Major G. de Hoghton, M.C., proceeded on leave to Paris.	033
			Rev. C. Hulmes, C.F., rejoined from Div.	
			Lt. ? R. Broadbent, 2/Lt. S.W. Downey and Guther rejoined from leave in U.K.	
			Coy. Training.	
			do	
	11th		Captain T.H.J. Upton rejoined from Divl. Rest Camp.	033

WAR DIARY / INTELLIGENCE SUMMARY

Army Form C. 2118.

1st K.O.Y.L.I. Vth Corps XXVI (Artist)
September 18. Sheet 2.

Place	Date	Hour	Summary of Events and Information	Remarks and references to Appendices
MARTIN EGLISE	12th		2/Lt. P.C. Scott and 2/Lt. H. Redfern rejoined from leave.	088
			Bn. on Coy. Training.	
	13th		*/Mr. J.G. Hudson rejoined from leave in U.K.	088
			Bn. on work.	
	14th		2/Lts. P.J. Hill and L.G. Whiting rejoined from leave.	088
	15th		Platoon and Coy. Training.	
	15th	11.30 a.m.	2/Lt. H.B. Fridge rejoined from Hospital. 2/Lt. J.R. Broadbent joined 13th Div. details in transit camp. MARTIN EGLISE and entrained at DIEPPE	088
	16th	2.25 a.m.	en route to 3rd Army Area.	088
	16th	6 a.m.	Bn. arrived at BOUQUEMAISON and marched to SUS ST LEGER. Bn. billeted in village.	088
SUS ST LEGER	17th		*/Mr. C.J. Sykes and W. Brown rejoined from leave.	088
			Major G. de Hoghton, M.C. rejoined from leave.	088
	18th		Lt. H.B. Postgate + B.Lt. J. Stead to.	
			Classes of instruction in L.G., + Scouting and Sniping commenced.	
	18th 19th 20th 21st		Bn. Training as usual.	088

WAR DIARY
or
INTELLIGENCE SUMMARY.

(Erase heading not required.)

Army Form C. 2118.

Volume XXVI (contd)
1st K.O.Y.L.I.
September 1918.
Sheet 3.

Instructions regarding War Diaries and Intelligence Summaries are contained in F. S. Regs., Part II. and the Staff Manual respectively. Title pages will be prepared in manuscript.

Place	Date	Hour	Summary of Events and Information	Remarks and references to Appendices
SUS. ST LEGER	22nd		Field Firing by Companies.	088
	23rd		Musketry and Coy. Training.	088
	24th		do.	088
	25th		Inspection of Bn. by Brig. Gen. R.S. Ryder, D.S.O.	088
	26th		Bn. entrained at 10.15 a.m. for move to 4th Army area, arrived RAINNEVILLE 2 p.m. and billeted in village.	088
	27th		Course of Instruction and training resumed.	088
	28th		Bn. moved to 3rd Corps Area near MORLU, entrained at 2 p.m. and arrived MORLU 10 p.m. and bivouacked for the night.	088

Lt. C.H. Hastings 10136 R.A.M.S. Attd. and 20133 Pte. T.E. Clarkson were mentioned in despatches for gallant conduct and distinguished service during period 25.9.17 to 28.2.18 (London Gazette 11.6.18).
2/Lt. P.R. Ross M.F. seconded 4.29.6.18 (London Gazette 2/8/18).
Lt. R. Murden R.War. Regt. returns retiring at eye deft. Capt. Whitell - comdg. 13. E.F. 2038.)
Lt. Y.K. Lambert to be acting Captain (adjt.) 9.8.18. (B.E.F. List - 2038.)
Capt. (temp. H. Col.) H. de Haylet M.C. relinquished his temp. rank (appt. Finland 1st Yorks. L.I. 29-8-18). (B.E.F. List No. 2038).

D. D. & L., London, E.C.
Wt. W1771/M2031 750,000 5/17 Sch. 52 Forms/C2118/14
(A8001)

Army Form C. 2118.

WAR DIARY
or
INTELLIGENCE SUMMARY.
(Erase heading not required.)

1st K.O.Y.L.I. Volume XXVI (Contd). September 1918. Sheet 4

Place	Date	Hour	Summary of Events and Information	Remarks and references to Appendices
			During month:—	
			Admitted to 2d. Ambulance 74. Rejoined from Hospital 44.	A/4
			Leave to U.K. — 15. Rejoined from Leave 37 B.	A/5
			U.K. — 31	A/6
			Reinforcements from U.K. — 12.	A/7
			To Command — 49	A/8
			Rejoined from Command — 14.	A/9
			To Div. Details MAR???EQUSE — 20	A/8
			To Nurses & Instructors — 14.	A/9
29			Transferred from D.L.I.	
30			Baths renewed in Brewery in vicinity of NOEUX-LES-MINES	

J.W. Sh---
Major
for Lt. Col.
Commdg 1st K.O.Y.L.I.

15/50

WAR DIARY. No 5

Mic's West
1st King's Own Yorkshire Light Infantry

October, 1918.

Volume —

O.42
5 sheets

Army Form C. 2118.

WAR DIARY
of
INTELLIGENCE SUMMARY.

(Erase heading not required.)

1st Bn The Kings Own Yorkshire Light Infantry

October 1918.

Instructions regarding War Diaries and Intelligence Summaries are contained in F. S. Regs., Part II. and the Staff Manual respectively. Title pages will be prepared in manuscript.

Place	Date	Hour	Summary of Events and Information	Remarks and references to Appendices
BOOMERANG WOOD	1st.		Bn marched to EPEHY arrived 8.30 p.m. VAUGHAN'S BANK	app
VAUGHAN'S BANK	2nd.	3.30 p.m	Bn moved in support to 140 W Bde in the HINDENBURG LINE - relieved 37th and 80th Bns Australian I.F. 2 ORs killed & 2 ORs wounded by shell on LEMPIRE-BONY Road	app
HINDENBURG LINE	3rd.		Bn moved to "jumping off" point to attack enemy objective - PROSPECT HILL - objective gained 10 a.m. - encountered heavy MG barrage. N.E. BONY. Casualties: Killed - Lieut. T.G.V. Ewings 2/Lt PJ. Hill - 42 ORanks. Wounded Major G de Hoghton M.C. Capt R Meadows (R War R) 2/Lt D. Shires, 2/Lt W Brown, 2/Lt T. Hagman, 2/Lt T.G. Hudson + 145 O.Ranks. Missing D.O. Ranks. Prisoners: 3 Officers 205 O.Ranks belonging to 114 Btn, 844 864, 86th Infantry Regts and Red Guards Regt	app
PROSPECT HILL	---	12 M.N	Relieved by 7th Wiltshire Regt moved to HINDENBURG LINE S. of BONY - Major G de Hoghton M.C. commanded the operations	app
HINDENBURG LINE	4th	9 a.m.	Major G. de Hoghton M/C & Capt R Meadows wounded previous day but remained with the Bn - 12.30 p.m. moved to take up defensive flank in the HINDENBURG LINE in vicinity ROCKY KNOLL 5 p.m. moved to support 2/R. Mus. Fus. in LE CATELET trench 7.15 p.m. Bn attacked RICHMOND COPSE - mopped up German trenches & M.G. Employments in the mountain - 4/K.R.R.C. & 2/R Mus Fus. consolidated Posts N. & W. RICHMOND COPSE. Casualties: 5 ORs wounded	app
RICHMOND COPSE	5th	11.0 p.m	Bn moved to HINDENBURG LINE S. BONY.	app
HINDENBURG LINE	6th	7 a.m.	Moved to GUILLAMONT FARM and bivouacked in HINDENBURG LINE	app
GUILLAMONT FARM	7th	4 p.m.	Moved to MACQUINCOURT Trench S. of VENDHUILE	app
MACQUINCOURT Trench	8th	0.100	Moved to GOUY. - Bn Headquarters in burnt house "B" and "D" Coy in burnt house "A" Coy 2nd wave. "C" Coy & "HQ Coy" 3rd wave.	app
GOUY.			Barrage opened - Dispositions. Objective gained by 0845 hours. - 1 section DOR Bn M.G.Coy supported the attack - FARM was stoutly held by Machine Guns	app

D. D. & L., London, E.C.
(A801) Wt. W.1771/M2091 750,000 5/17 Sch. 52 Forms/Ca118/14

WAR DIARY or INTELLIGENCE SUMMARY

Army Form C. 2118.

October 1918 Sheet 11

1st Bn The King's Own Yorkshire Light Infantry

Place	Date	Hour	Summary of Events and Information	Remarks and references to Appendices
Villers Farm	8th (contd)		both heavy & light. Casualties 2/Lt P.C. Scott - Killed, 2/Lt K. Robinson Wounded, 7 ORs Killed, 24 ORs Wounded. Prisoners 1 Offr & 8 ORs unwounded, 1 OR wounded. Captain A.G. Storing commanded the operations. AR is still in influenza.	ags
	9th		Hostile aircraft bombed bivouac area - no casualties - during night	ags
Vaucelles Quarry	10th		Vaucelles Quarry - Col. J. Mallinson D.S.O. returned. During period 3rd to 8th inst. Bn. captured. 4 light Trench Mortars & 30 M.Gs	ags
"	11th	10.30	Vaucelles Quarry Command of the Battalion from Commanding Offr. Battle Surplus.	ags
Maretz	12th		Entrained Goy for MARETZ, arrived 1300 hours	ags
Maretz	13th		" Battle Surplus rejoined Bn. 2nd Lt. J. Wheatcroft joined for Bns. Genl. R.C. Sugden D.S.O. (unposted) (Bn.)	ags
"	14th			
"	15th			
"	"	1500	Remained in Billets until 1500 hours.	ags
"	"		Marched to ESCAUFORT, bivouacked for the night preparatory to attacking enemy position along River SELLE.	
Escaufort	16th	1200	Bn. moved to assembly position about 800x N. of ST. SOUPLET - objective WASSIGNY - LE CATEAU ROAD - from the BRICKFIELDS to a point about 800x S.E. Some difficulty was experienced crossing the River SELLE, this was done by means of small portable wooden bridges.	ags
Assembly Point	17th	0530	Action opened, 3 minute later filed in to the Railway line - crossing of the men commenced - there was a dense fog at the time - Disposition "B" Coy on the Rt "A" Coy on the left. "C" Coy in Support & "D" Coy in Reserve. "D" Coy leaving the task of mopping up the DETRAINING POINT. The enemy Artillery which had been active in about an hour before ceased as soon as crossing the River and the high ground West of it - the objective was attained with little loss - the advance against the Railway	ags

Army Form C. 2118.

WAR DIARY
or
INTELLIGENCE SUMMARY.
(Erase heading not required.)

1st Bn. The Kings Own Yorkshire Light Infantry

OCTOBER 1918
Sheet III

Place	Date	Hour	Summary of Events and Information	Remarks and references to Appendices
Railway Emb.	17th	06:15	Line was met with strong resistance from Machine Guns & Rifles & Snipers. The Railway Embankment was captured at 06:15 hours. Companies then moved down the Eastern side of the Railway line towards their objective. Of the stage body was kept till the 4th K.R.R.C. & 6th R.Innis.Fus. but later owing to the mist & heavy casualties	App
Objective	17th	10:00	sustained he lost touch with 6th R.Innis Fus. – operating on the WASSIGNY – LE CATEAU Road was checked at about 10:00 hours. It was now ascertained by patrols that there was a large gap in the line between our left Company & the 6th R.Innis who were still on the line of the Railway Embankment in the neighbourhood of the DETRAINING POINT. A local enemy counter attack forced "C" "D" Coys back to the Railway line with the assistance of a section of Vickers Guns and held on all day until the 2nd Royal Dublin Fus. moved up about 4pm & closed the gap. "A" "B" "C" "D" Coys having been supplied with ammunition used up into the neighbourhood of the	App
	17th	10:00	DETRAINING POINT.— About 10:00 hours orders were received that the 2nd R.Dub.Fus. and 2nd R.Innis.Fus. with 1st K.O.Y.L.I. operating under Comand of Lt. Colonel H. NANCARROW, D.S.O., were to take the objective. The operation	App
Detraining Pt.	18th	05:30	was carried out during the night and the line was held.	App
—			O.450 hrs, advance was made to a line 700 x E of BASUEL, which was reached by 07:30 hours.	
—			Here Bn. held on. O.730 hours a Bde. of the 25th Division passed thro' Bn. and continued the advance. Be. withdrew to the WASSIGNY – LE CATEAU Road – remained here until	App
Wassigny – Le Cateau Rd	19th	12:00	18:00 hours.	App
			Moved to Billets in AVELU. arrived 18:00 hours. Casualties since 18th Oct. F.G. SCOTT killed. Lt. O'TOOLE E.York R att Killed. Lt. C.A.R. BROMHAM. Devon Regt. Wounded. Lt. F. FRANKLIN, Lt. C.R. ROEBUCK 2/Lt L.M. GAZE O.Ranks 14. Capt. T.F.T. Upton (remained at duty) Wounded 40 O.Ranks	App
Avelu	20th		O.Ranks 123. Prisoners – approximately 200.	App
—	21st		in billets. Bn. inspected by Brig. Gen. R.B. Sugden D.S.O.	App
—	22nd		– " – 2/Lt S.W. Downes & 19th Corps & Maj Gen. H.C. Jackson D.S.O. of Marti. Bn inspected by	App
—	23rd		– " – 2/Lts H. Cockayne & J.S. Brooks Joined Bn. 323 O.R.s joined from U.K.	App
—	24th		– " – from T.E.E. Pasford M.C. The Kings Own Regt reported from Hosp.	App
	Rum		2/Lts H. Haldsworth & R. Brook joined from U.K. In Billets. M.J.L. Shipman-Burnett and L. joined Bn. O.Ranks joined Bn.	App

Army Form C. 2118.

WAR DIARY
or
INTELLIGENCE SUMMARY.
(Erase heading not required.)

OCTOBER 1918. Sheet No IV
1st Bn The King's Own Yorkshire Light Infantry

Place	Date	Hour	Summary of Events and Information	Remarks and references to Appendices
AVENU	25th		In Billets	ass
AVENU	26th		In Billets	ass
"	27th		" "	ass
"	28th		" "	ass
"	29th		11.30 hours Bn marched to MAUROIS arrived 12.30 hours - billeted for the night	ass
MAUROIS	30th	1430	Bn marched to LE CATEAU arrived 1700 hours - billeted for the night	ass
LE CATEAU	31st		In Billets. Bde in Divnl Reserve	
			Honours & Awards :-	
			9278 Sergt Lu Hooley } Awarded Military Medal for	
			9732 Sergt. A G Smith } Gallantry during operations	
			Centre killed in action PROSPECT HILL - HILLERS FARM	
			Sick wastage during month 101 68 ORs	
			Battle Casualties Killed 6 57 "	
			Wounded Gassed 12 274 "	
			Missing 1 3 "	
			Died of Disease - 40 "	
			Reinforcements 5 419 ORs	

Nov 1st. 10.18.

M. M. Mullen
Lieut. Colonel
Commanding 1st Bn The King's Own Yorkshire Light Infantry.

WAR DIARY.

1st Bn. King's Own Yorkshire Light Infantry

November, 1918.

Vol 6

Volume —

O.43

? Fôt S.T AUBIN — AVESNES
road AVESNES-MAUBEUGE
                    7th
                15/6/38.

Army Form C. 2118.

WAR DIARY
INTELLIGENCE SUMMARY

(Erase heading not required.)   1st Bn The Kings Own Yorkshire Light Infantry

NOVEMBER 1918.   Sheet 1.

Place	Date	Hour	Summary of Events and Information	Remarks and references to Appendices
LE CATEAU	1st		In Billets.	
"	2nd		- do -	
"	3rd		- do - 00.30 hours Bn marched to ROUSIES.	
ROUSIES	4th	06.15	Bn "Stand To". 07.45 a.m. marched on	
FONTAINE-AU-BOIS		10.30	The Bn. were ordered to pass through the 150th Inf Bde who had gained their objective in the FOREST DE MORMAL. At an hotel by the ROUTE DE FONTAINE through the Forest meeting a considerable amount of opposition from enemy machine gun fire. The enemy retired on front of the Bn until dark to a point in the vicinity of ROUTE DU PONT ROUTIER, Bn. dug in for night.	
ROUTE DU PONT ROUTIER 5th		04.00	The attack resumed, Bn crossed positions in the Bde line from left flank. 07.30 attack commenced objective - HACHETTE FARM - advanced 1000yds. 149 Inf Bde passed through Bn at about midday & concentrated for the night in the neighbourhood of HACHETTE FARM.	
HACHETTE FARM	6th	13.30	Bn marched to NOYELLES & billeted for the night	
NOYELLES	7th	05.30	Bn left NOYELLES with orders to advance through the 149 Inf Bde who were holding a position near ST REMY CHAUSSEE, and to advance to the ST AUBIN-AVESNES ROAD. This met however impossible at the time owing to the strong resistance met with near DOURLERS 1000 yards short of the objective.	
DOURLERS	8th	07.30	The attack was resumed objective ST AUBIN-AVESNES ROAD. This was reached 09.30 hours in spite of	

Army Form C. 2118.

WAR DIARY
INTELLIGENCE SUMMARY

NOVEMBER 1918   Sheet II

1st Bn. The King's Own Yorkshire Light Infantry.

(Erase heading not required.)

Instructions regarding War Diaries and Intelligence Summaries are contained in F. S. Regs., Part II. and the Staff Manual respectively. Title pages will be prepared in manuscript.

Place	Date	Hour	Summary of Events and Information	Remarks and references to Appendices
DOURLERS	8th	Continued:	Enemy Machine Gun Fire. Position held although shelled very heavily until the Scottish Horse passed through us about 1515 hours. During the night, the enemy country attacked but were repulsed.	
MONCHEAU	9th	1300	Bn. with drums to MONCHEAU. Billeted for the night in Barns.	
ST. REMY CHAUSSÉE	10th	1500	Bn. marched to ST. REMY CHAUSSÉE. Billeted for the night. 2/Lt J.W. B.C. Handcock rejoined.	
MONCHEAU	11th		Bn. returned to Barns neighbourhood MONCHEAU.	
"	12th		In Billets. Bn Headquarters moved to billets in village.	
"	13th		" "	
"	14th		Bn. Parade. Divnl Commander present Medal Ribbons: Military Cross: Captain O.E. Stobey, Capt. W. Bailey, 2/Lt. B. Podeloot. Bar to D.C.M.: 6801 R.S.M.Q. Dillon D.C.M. D.C.M.: 91281 C.S.M. F.C. Fraser. Military Medal: 8-4-4-9- 96. Storey. C.I. 13-4-9 & Bailey, W.	
"	15th		In Billets.	
"	16th to 19th		In Billets.	
"	20th to 22nd		Bn. employed on Salvage work in vicinity of MONCHEAU ST. WAAST, ST LEVEQUE and SASSEGNIES.	
"	23rd to 29th		In the morning Coy Training - Afternoon Recreational Training.	
"	30th		Justice Parade for H.M. the King's visit to the 50th Divisional Area.	

Casualties.

Army Form C. 2118.

Sheet No III

WAR DIARY
or
INTELLIGENCE SUMMARY.

(Erase heading not required.)

1st Bn the Kings Own Yorkshire Light Infantry

November 1918.

Instructions regarding War Diaries and Intelligence Summaries are contained in F.S. Regs., Part II. and the Staff Manual respectively. Title pages will be prepared in manuscript.

Place	Date	Hour	Summary of Events and Information	Remarks and references to Appendices
			Casualties during the month:-	
			KILLED: Capt. T.F.J. Upton. Lieut. C.W. Telfer. Lieut. G.H. Nelligan. 2nd Lieut. A. Brook	
			Other ranks 25.	
			WOUNDED: Capt. H.W. Hyne. 2nd Lieut. T.W. St Leger-Russell. Lieut. H.B. Judge.	
			Other ranks 132	
			MISSING: Other ranks 4.	
			GASSED:- Other ranks 3	
			Total Officers 7 Other ranks 165	
			Honours & Rewards.	
			D.S.O. = Capt.(a/Major) G. de Hoghton M.C.	✓
			Military Crosses:- Lt. (a/Capt) Q.S. Stenning. Lieut.(a/Capt) H.W. Hyne. Lieut.(a/Capt) H.B. Notley	✓
			Lieut B. Lonsdale. Lieut. W. Tomkin	
			Bar to D.C.M.:- 6401 R.S.M. G. Miles D.C.M.	✓
			D.C.M's:- 6788 C.S.M. F.C. Thorley. 8767 C.S.M. C. Cook	✓
			Bar to M.M:- 9278 Sergt. J.W. Wooley	✓
			Military Medals: 18.	✓
			Reinforcements: Officers 8. Other Ranks 132.	✓
			Sick Wastage: Officers 2. Other Ranks 58.	✓
			Sports:- Football - Inter Platoon Knock Out Competition; Winners No 2 Platoon "B" Coy. Runners Up No 10 Platoon "C" Coy.	✓
			Officers - Reinforcements. Lost	
			2.5.21. C.S. Cope. 18.11.18 Lt. G. Hepworth Capt. G.W. Jepson M.C.	
			9.11. 2/Lt St C. Hendriks. 21st. Capt. H.W. Hyne M.C.	
			2nd Lt. P. Stanton. Wounded 25.11.18.	
			22.11. O.B.L.I. Officers att. 2/Lt. H.T. Olsen R. S.S. Maguire G.E. Paresons	
			Lt. J. Kincaid M.C. J.H. Kinghorn	

Commanding 1st Bn K.O.Y.L.I. Lt. Colonel.

WAR DIARY

1st Bn THE KING'S OWN YORKSHIRE LIGHT INFANTRY

DECEMBER 1918.

WAR DIARY
or
INTELLIGENCE SUMMARY.

(Erase heading not required.) 10/8 BR. THE KINGS OWN YORKSHIRE LIGHT INFANTRY.

Army Form C. 2118.
SHEET 1.

DECEMBER 1918.

Place	Date 1918	Hour	Summary of Events and Information	Remarks and references to Appendices
Monceau	Dec 1		S.A.A.G.	
			Lt B. Ashford was appointed fighter Anti-Gas Officer. Ady 23-11-18 (List N 26)	ref
			2/Lt G.E. Pearson (R.E.F.) admitted to Hosp.	ref
	3		Lt A.J. Mitchell M.C. Nominal roll of officers - orders and strength returns rendered to Records.	ref
	5		The Bn moved to MAUBEUGE by march route Casting MONCEAU 10:30AM - arriving ROUTES X ROADS - PONT - Noon ST REMY, Billets Road through PONT SUR SAMBRE. - Billets good instable	ref
	9		Capt. W.C. Jouce, one of 1st O.T.C. joined the Bn - Posted to A.Coy and assumed Command vice Capt S. Bradshaw M.C.	ref
	10		W.D.J.E. Rawlings joined from U.K.	ref
	12		2/Lt S.G. White Transferred to 19th K.R.D.L.	ref
			Capt H.E. Scott reposted to B. Coy vice Comdr	
			Capt Bradshaw M.C. assumed Command of A Coy	
	15		A meeting of representatives of the R of B Coy's unit to the C.M. MENDYCHES re the Bn Xmas	ref
			Held at Mess 3:30. It was decided to purchase at MONS 80 turkeys, 80lbs and 40 others	
			Suitable eg... Et the Xmas of the Rees and tea to commence at the Men	
	17		Chas. parading prescribed on date (Compros)	
	18		Gen Paris as follows forenoon parade ... to depot to Carrier, the Glen Park of the Regt.	ref
			Gen A. O. Truckly M.C. Capt. A. Chambert. Rev J. Kelly, Item 290 Etc samedent approached	
			M. Usal Roprils took place Command and Inspection of H Coy by C.O. left afternoon	
	28		Gen Casy by Run - April 930, the Romans H.O.Coy ... County Cup - D.	ref
	29		Lt. C.H. Hastings Procesed on leave	ref
	26		2/Lt G.T. Allen (Continued)	ref

D. D. & L. London, E.C.
(A801) Wt. W1771/M2091 750,000 5/17 Sch. 52 Forms,C2118/14

Army Form C. 2118.

WAR DIARY
or
INTELLIGENCE SUMMARY.

(Erase heading not required.) 1st Bn. THE KINGS OWN YORKSHIRE LIGHT INFANTRY.

DECEMBER 1918. Page 11.

Place	Date	Hour	Summary of Events and Information	Remarks and references to Appendices
MEAULTE	Dec 13.		John Norman and W.J.Smith C.S.M. awarded M.M. by the Corp Comdg.	
	Dec 3		10,309,29 Sgt Ferman S. and 200563 L/C. Halligan P. awarded D.M.M by M/Gen. Solloy's operations in the Royal Artos. Consolidated.	
	Dec 28		Educational schemes commenced — Estimated Bookkeeping, Shorthand, English & Educational Lectures. French Algebra Geometry Inclusive.	
	" 11		Tractors M/Majors, 2nd G.S.pls, W/C.Sgts, Q/M.Sgts nee, Rev S.A. Wilkinson Lieut G.F.T. Gilbert performed the Duties for Bn. Educational Officer pro tem.	
	" 30		Evacuated to Hospital 24 O.R.a to Reinforcements. 99.	

31/3/18

W. Atkinson Lt Col
Comdg 1 KOYLI

WAR DIARY

1st Bn. The Kings Own Yorkshire Light Infantry

January 1919.

Vol. 50

WAR DIARY
or
INTELLIGENCE SUMMARY.
(Erase heading not required.)

Army Form C. 2118.

JANUARY 1919. Vol. 50
SHEET I
1/5 Bn. THE KINGS OWN YORKSHIRE LIGHT INFTY

Place	Date	Hour	Summary of Events and Information	Remarks and references to Appendices
MECQUINIES	Jan 1st		Bn. will B. 1. O.R. to base for Demobilisation. Bn. inspected by Bde. Genl. R.E. Sugden D.S.O. who said Good Bye to the Bn. on his leaving the Bde.	A.L.
	2			A.L.
	3		Lt Col Y. Ivinson D.S.O. proceeded to 151 Bde. HQ. to Command Bde. Maj. I.E.E. Packard M.C. assumed Command of the Bn.	A.L.
	5		Colou (2 ORs returned from England. Colou's left at Base K.B. 1 OR & 2 OR Other ranks A.L. (Capt. W.T. Umbers, M.C. Capt F.R. Lambert, 5 Other ranks Dems Leave & other ranks, chat'n nat'n)	A.L.
	6		1 OR to UK for demob. 319 W. Honoured T.F. ORs reported from 157 T.M. Bty.	A.L.
	8		740 S.S. Whitley M.C. to UK. 14 days leave.	A.L.
	9th		Bandmaster Batson, MSStang, No Strang (including 23 boys) arrived from U.K.	
	13	1000	Commanded parade at B.H.Q PS Gutton carried the King's Colour 2nd Lt P.S Gutton carried the Reg'tl Colour. Off'rs who had been received Mil. Sev'c. H.G. Jackson D.S.O presented with medal ribbons as follows: Capt H/Lt. E. M.C. 23392 A/Cpl Welbourn 70. 35103 Pte Coleman W. Lt 311 Pte King R.D. 0340 Sgt Cote L.S. 3502 Pte Peck J.I. 9519. Sgt Cutler J. E. 10101 Pte Whitehead A. 32950 Pte Wales R.E. 2182 Sgt Tate L.S. 8892. Pte Ruspen J. M.M's. Lee. Cpl Hastings and S.W Downey from leave. 6 ORs to UK for demob.	A.L.
	14			A.L.
	15			A.L.
	17		Capt. R. & Sgt H. Wilkinson M.C. and 10 ORs to U.K. for demob. Lt Col Downey resumed command.	A.L.
	18		Lt Col C/ Capt R.F Standing M.C. on leave to UK. Capt F.R. Lambert assumed command of Capt.	A.L.
	19		2nd Lt Davies Eh. R.M. returned from 157 T.M Bty and received command	A.L.
	20		Capt Newns L.g a new weekly instructive and interesting lecture on Demobilisation and Reconstruction, Being most ably attended by all ranks. 5 ORs to UK for demob.	A.L.
	21st		Capt. & W.A. Todd M.T. A Sports Offr and York Fu.R. for demob. 29 ORs to UK demob.	A.L.
			Command Chr'd A.R.C.	
	22	0920	Bn. Route Jun'cl.	A.L.
	23		Capt. N.B. McColl ? & M.C. add. to UK leave. MSE.SUGNIES, LOUVIGNIES, AUNAIS LOUVIGNIES	A.L.
	24		Capt H.W Murby M.C. 12 Sgts 12 ORs to UK for demob. Lt Col Jones assumed command	A.L.
				T.D.C.4

Army Form C. 2118.

WAR DIARY
or
INTELLIGENCE SUMMARY.

(Erase heading not required.)

January 1919. Sheet II

1/5 Bn. The King's Own Yorkshire Light Infty.

Instructions regarding War Diaries and Intelligence Summaries are contained in F. S. Regs., Part II. and the Staff Manual respectively. Title pages will be prepared in manuscript.

Place	Date 1919	Hour	Summary of Events and Information	Remarks and references to Appendices
MECQUIGNIES	Jan 24		Maj. J.E.E. PACKARD. M.C. on leave to U.K.	
	24		Capt. H.S. LYNE M.C and 18 O.Rs. to U.K. and Capt. 7/4.S. Wheatcroft assumed command O/C Coy. Theo. G. Whiting M.C. returned from leave and assumed Command of B. Coy.	
	29.	15.30	Bn. furnished a Guard of Honour. 3 offrs and 100 O.Rs. King's Colour and Band, to President POINCARE at POIX-YZ. Capt H.P Kentish in command. Major Stanton carried the King's Colour	
			Lt.Col. C.R.I. BROOKE CMG. DSO took over command of the 2nd Bn. and proceeded to take command of the 2nd Bn.	
	31		Following honours were notified in the New Year's Despatch.	
			Capt. E.L. WHEELWRIGHT. OBE.	
			Capt. H.B. McCOLL. R.A.M.C. acq OBE.	
			Following are numbers of Re-enlistments during the month under P.O.W. of 9, 10 Dec 1918. 4yrs. 3yrs. 2yrs.	
			Sgts. 2. 1. - Total 18.	
			O.Rs. 11. 5. -	
			Following proceeded to U.K. during month for Demobilisation. Offrs 5. O.Rs. 70. (includes 6 other Ranks)	
			Evacuated to Hosp. 25. O.Rs.	
			Reinforcements. 2. offrs. 49 O.Rs. (includes 10 offrs and 8 O.Rs from ----M.I.)	
			Educational work has proceeded satisfactorily throughout the month, and the teaching staff has been reduced by the demobilisation of 7/Lt Sykes and 9/Lt Cartr. All the boys attend school every evening 1.3 of them are candidates for 1st Class Certificates.	
			9/Lt Jones is secretary. The duties of Bn. Educational Officer are now 9/Lt Pilkington. On leave to U.K. pending demobilisation.	

Wheelwright
Comdg 1/5 Bn K.O.Y.L.I.

CONFIDENTIAL

WAR DIARY

1ST KINGSOWN (YORKSHIRE LIGHT INFANTRY)

1ST to 28TH FEBRUARY, 1919.

VOLUME LI.

WAR DIARY or INTELLIGENCE SUMMARY

Army Form C. 2118.

February 1919. SHEET 1.

1st Bn. THE KINGS OWN (YORKSHIRE LIGHT INFANTRY)

Place	Date	Hour	Summary of Events and Information	Remarks and references to Appendices
MECQUIGNIES	1.2.19.		In Billets.	
	6		Capt. PRESTON M.C. from leave UK	
	10		RSM MEW OBE MM RAMS from leave UK	
	15		Major J.S. McLEOD M.C. from leave UK.	
	19		2/Lt W. NORRIS arrived No. 3 CCS.	
			Lt Col CRAYFORD BROOKS CMG DSO to command 150 Inf. Bde.	
			Major J.S. PACKARD M.C. assumes command of the Battn.	
LOUVIGNIES LEZ 23			Capt. H.E. MCGILL OBE M.C. proceeded to UK course of Instruction in Surgery	
QUESNOY	25		Lt KAUR U.S.A. assumes position as M.O. the Battn.	
	26		The Battn. proceeded to change of area by march route (LOUVIGNIES-LEZ-QUESNOY).	
	27		Marched at various wind and bitter 14 Ms. Arrived at new billets in good billets area. Considerable damage had been done to billets by shell fire.	
	28		2/Lt McDERMOTT admitted 138 Field Amb.	
	26		2/Lt's Oblin M.C, Scarborough, Cope, J Brooks, D. Moyes, Y.P. Stanton, (M.T. absent), Lt Higgins, No McQueen, O.B.M. and Lt Rawfe proceeded to 2 O.K.C.H.T. - Draft entrance requisite Class at W Sthr.	
			2/Lt J.G. Rawlings East of UK (Contravenant) Demobilised Monmouth 137 O.R. to W. Bt.Pn. Reinforcements Y.O.R. to hosp. 16 O.R. Regt. owing to lack of suitable billets, Encamped Classes have unfortunately 150 outposts. Over the arrival of the Battn. in their area.	

28-2-1919.

J. Packard Major.
Comdg. 1st K.O.Y.L.I.

WAR DIARY

Volume 52

March 1919

1st Bn Kings Own Yorkshire L.Inf:

Army Form C. 2118.
SHEET 1

WAR DIARY
or
INTELLIGENCE SUMMARY.
(Erase heading not required.) or 2nd Bn. The King's Own (Yorkshire Light Infantry)

VOL. 52. MARCH 1919.

Place	Date	Hour	Summary of Events and Information	Remarks and references to Appendices
LONGUENESSE LEZ QUESNOY	March 1		In Billets. The Bn. was preparing to move 2 Coys. to area bgd. (2nd Lt. L.S.C. Kendrick) and duty Coy (Lt. A.W. Dowler). However it was found that it was not required.	ass
	6		Temporary Process for duty of 2/Lt. P. O'N. Coy. Rosser.	ass
	10		Rev. Jas. Dickinson (CF cease) to be attached 2nd H.H.P.R.C.	ass
	10		Bn. Hospital note 1 6/- and commanded by Lt. L.S.C. Kendricks	ass
	21		Lt. W. Noumi married. To UK sick.	ass
	23		Lt. Col. Ralph Booth CMG DSO assumed command 1st 151st Inf. Bde.	ass
	22		Major Booth CMG DSO relinquish command of 150th Inf. Bde.	ass
	27		L.Sgt. G. Kendricks leave to UK. (6 days)	
	28		Lt. Col. R.B. Booth CMG DSO, and Lt. Maj. Stoned proceed on leave to UK (14 days)	ass
			To Hospital during the month .... 3 ORs	
			To Command .... " .... 1 "	
			From .... " .... 16 "	
			Posted (OR) .... " .... 16 "	
			To Demobilisation & Furlough .... 16 "	
			To UK for duty (Military Affairs) ...... 2 "	
			Honours and Rewards.	
			No 10263 Sgt. Tighe F. (att. 151st T.M. Batty.)	
			" 9998 Sgt Iveson J.	
			Awarded the Military Medal for Gallantry and devotion to duty.	
			1=4-19	[signature] E.E. Maclean Major Comdg. 1st Bn. KOYLI

Army Form C. 2118.

WAR DIARY
or
INTELLIGENCE SUMMARY.
(Erase heading not required.)

Vol. 53. April 1919.

Sheet One.

1st.Bn.The King's Own Yorkshire Light Infantry.

Place	Date	Hour	Summary of Events and Information	Remarks and references to Appendices
LOUVIGNIES LEZ QUESNOY.	1		Bn in billets in LOUVIGNIES LEZ QUESNOY, Nord. Strength, 4 officers and 105 other ranks.	
	2		Brig-Gen.M.Minshull Ford relinquished command of 151st.Infy.Bde.	
	4		2/Lt.M.Holdsworth rejoined from hospital and proceeded to base for demobilization.	
	5		Cadre of 2nd.Bn.(Lt.Col.H.Mallinson,D.S.O. commanding) strength 6 officers and 86 other ranks, arrived from the Rhine and billeted in Louvignies.	
	9		Regimental equipment,Stores etc.,handed over to 2nd.Bn.	
	13		Lt.& Qr.Mr. S.Stroud rejoined from leave.	
			Lt.Col.C.R.Ingham Brooke,C.M.G.,D.S.O.,granted 2 months leave in U.K. under W.O.Letter.	
	19		Captain F.K.Lambert proceeded on 14 days leave.	
	25		Draft of 26 O.Rs.proceeded to 130th.Prisoners of War Camp at HAVRE for duty.	
	26		Major J.E.E.Packard,M.C., 2nd.King's Own (R.L.) Regt.,proceeded on 14 days Special leave.	
	28		14 other ranks proceeded to 1st/5th Bn.K.O.S.B.,Eastern Division, posted for duty.	
			Bn. became reduced to Cadre strength.	
	30		Strength, 5 officers and 60 other ranks.	
			To base for demob. 13. To command 10. To hospital,sick,2.	
			do repatriation 1. From do 14. From do 2.	
			do R.A.O.C. 2. To 1/5th.Bn.I. Reinforcements 4.	
			Leave to U.K. 22. To re-enlistment furlo' 2.	
			From Leave 4.	

[signature]
Captain.
Commanding 1st.Bn.The King's Own Yorkshire Light Infantry.

Volume 54. WAR DIARY 1/4 The King's Own Yorkshire Light Infantry
or
INTELLIGENCE SUMMARY. Sheet 1.

Army Form C. 2118.

MAY 1919

Place	Date 1919	Hour	Summary of Events and Information	Remarks and references to Appendices
Louvignies les Quesnoy.	May 1.		Cadre in Billets. Strength 30 Officers and 54 O. Ranks.	ass
	6		Capt. A.F. Lambert rejoined from leave (UK)	ass
	11		Lt. C.P. Hastings proceeded on leave UK.	ass
			Proceeded U.K. on leave 3 O.Rs. Rejoined from " 6 " Posted to 2nd Bn 4 " To Hospt. Sick 3 " From Hospt. 1 "	ass
	31.		Strength 30 Officers 54 O. Ranks.	

A. Stanbury, Captain
t/ K.O.Y.L.I.
Comdg.

www.ingramcontent.com/pod-product-compliance
Lightning Source LLC
Chambersburg PA
CBHW081456160426
43193CB00013B/2504